This NoteBook Belongs To:

DATE: /   /

____

TOP 3 THINGS ABOUT TODAY

○ ___________________________________
○ ___________________________________
○ ___________________________________

WHAT EMOTIONS HAVE YOU FELT TODAY?

HOW WOULD YOU RATE THE DAY?

☆ ☆ ☆ ☆ ☆

WHAT INSPIRED YOU THE MOST TODAY?

3 THINGS I WISH FOR TOMORROW

○ ___________________________________
○ ___________________________________
○ ___________________________________

DATE: /   /

WO RISKS. WO MAGIC

TOP 3 THIGS ABOUT TODAY
○ _________________________
○ _________________________
○ _________________________

WHAT EMOTIONS HAVE YOU FELT TODAY

HOW WOULD YOU RATE THE DAY

WHAT INSPIRED YOU THE MOST TODAY

3 THINGS I WISH FOR TOMORROW
○ _________________________
○ _________________________
○ _________________________

DATE: /   /

NO RISKS. NO MAGIC

TOP 3 THINGS ABOUT TODAY

○

○

○

WHAT EMOTIONS HAVE YOU FELT TODAY?

HOW WOULD YOU RATE THE DAY?

WHAT INSPIRED YOU THE MOST TODAY?

3 THINGS I WISH FOR TOMORROW

○

○

○

DATE: /   /

NO RISKS, NO MAGIC

TOP 3 THINGS ABOUT TODAY
○ ____________________
○ ____________________
○ ____________________

WHAT INSPIRED YOU THE MOST TODAY?

WHAT EMOTIONS HAVE YOU FELT TODAY?

3 THINGS I WISH FOR TOMORROW
○ ____________________
○ ____________________
○ ____________________

HOW WOULD YOU RATE THE DAY?
☆ ☆ ☆ ☆ ☆

DATE: /   /

TOP 3 THIGS ABOUT TODAY
○ _______________________
○ _______________________
○ _______________________

WHAT EMOTIONS HAVE YOU FELT TODAY?

HOW WOULD YOU RATE THE DAY

WHAT INSPIRED YOU THE MOST TODAY?

3 THINGS I WISH FOR TOMORROW
○ _______________________
○ _______________________
○ _______________________

DATE: /   /

NO RISKS. NO MAGIC

TOP 3 THIGS ABOUT TODAY
○
○
○

WHAT EMOTIONS HAVE YOU FELT TODAY

HOW WOULD YOU RATE THE DAY

WHAT INSPIRED YOU THE MOST TODAY

3 THINGS I WISH FOR TOMORROW
○
○
○

____
____
____
____
____
____

____
____
____
____

NO RISKS. NO MAGIC

TOP 3 THINGS ABOUT TODAY

○ _______________________________
○ _______________________________
○ _______________________________

WHAT EMOTIONS HAVE YOU FELT TODAY?
____

HOW WOULD YOU RATE THE DAY?
____
☆ ☆ ☆ ☆ ☆

WHAT INSPIRED YOU THE MOST TODAY?

3 THINGS I WISH FOR TOMORROW

____
○ _______________________________
○ _______________________________
○ _______________________________

DATE: /   /

TOP 3 THINGS ABOUT TODAY
○
○
○

WHAT EMOTIONS HAVE YOU FELT TODAY?

HOW WOULD YOU RATE THE DAY?
☆ ☆ ☆ ☆ ☆

WHAT INSPIRED YOU THE MOST TODAY?

3 THINGS I WISH FOR TOMORROW
○
○
○

DATE: /   /

NO RISKS. NO MAGIC

TOP 3 THINGS ABOUT TODAY
○ ______________________________
○ ______________________________
○ ______________________________

WHAT EMOTIONS HAVE YOU FELT TODAY!

HOW WOULD YOU RATE THE DAY!

☆ ☆ ☆ ☆ ☆

WHAT INSPIRED YOU THE MOST TODAY!

3 THINGS I WISH FOR TOMORROW
○ ______________________________
○ ______________________________
○ ______________________________

DATE: /   /

NO RISKS. NO MAGIC

TOP 3 THINGS ABOUT TODAY
○
○
○

WHAT INSPIRED YOU THE MOST TODAY?

WHAT EMOTIONS HAVE YOU FELT TODAY?

3 THINGS I WISH FOR TOMORROW
○
○
○

HOW WOULD YOU RATE THE DAY?
☆ ☆ ☆ ☆ ☆

DATE: /   /

NO RISKS. NO MAGIC

TOP 3 THIGS ABOUT TODAY
○
○
○

WHAT INSPIRED YOU THE MOST TODAY?

WHAT EMOTIONS HAVE YOU FELT TODAY?

3 THINGS I WISH FOR TOMORROW
○
○
○

HOW WOULD YOU RATE THE DAY?

DATE   /   /

NO RISKS. NO MAGIC

TOP 3 THINGS ABOUT TODAY
○
○
○

WHAT INSPIRED YOU THE MOST TODAY?

WHAT EMOTIONS HAVE YOU FELT TODAY?

3 THINGS I WISH FOR TOMORROW
○
○
○

HOW WOULD YOU RATE THE DAY?

☆ ☆ ☆ ☆ ☆

DATE: /   /

NO RISKS. NO MAGIC

TOP 3 THINGS ABOUT TODAY
○
○
○

WHAT INSPIRED YOU THE MOST TODAY!

WHAT EMOTIONS HAVE YOU FELT TODAY!

3 THINGS I WISH FOR TOMORROW
○
○
○

HOW WOULD YOU RATE THE DAY!

☆ ☆ ☆ ☆ ☆

DATE: /   /

WO RISKS. WO MAGIC

TOP 3 THINGS ABOUT TODAY
○ ______________________
○ ______________________
○ ______________________

WHAT INSPIRED YOU THE MOST TODAY?

WHAT EMOTIONS HAVE YOU FELT TODAY?

3 THINGS I WISH FOR TOMORROW

HOW WOULD YOU RATE THE DAY?

☆ ☆ ☆ ☆ ☆

○ ______________________
○ ______________________
○ ______________________

DATE: /   /

NO RISKS. NO MAGIC

____

TOP 3 THIGS ABOUT TODAY

○ _____________________________________

○ _____________________________________

○ _____________________________________

WHAT INSPIRED YOU THE MOST TODAY

WHAT EMOTIONS HAVE YOU FELT TODAY

3 THINGS I WISH FOR TOMORROW

○ _____________________________________

○ _____________________________________

○ _____________________________________

HOW WOULD YOU RATE THE DAY

☆ ☆ ☆ ☆ ☆

DATE: /   /

NO RISKS, NO MAGIC

TOP 3 THINGS ABOUT TODAY
○
○
○

WHAT INSPIRED YOU THE MOST TODAY?

WHAT EMOTIONS HAVE YOU FELT TODAY?

3 THINGS I WISH FOR TOMORROW
○
○
○

HOW WOULD YOU RATE THE DAY?
☆ ☆ ☆ ☆ ☆

DATE: /   /

WO RISKS. WO MAGIC

TOP 3 THIGS ABOUT TODAY
○ ___________________________
○ ___________________________
○ ___________________________

WHAT INSPIRED YOU THE MOST TODAY!

WHAT EMOTIONS HAVE YOU FELT TODAY!

3 THINGS I WISH FOR TOMORROW
○ ___________________________
○ ___________________________
○ ___________________________

HOW WOULD YOU RATE THE DAY!
☆ ☆ ☆ ☆ ☆

TOP 3 THIGS ABOUT TODAY

○
○
○

WHAT EMOTIONS HAVE YOU FELT TODAY

HOW WOULD YOU RATE THE DAY

WHAT INSPIRED YOU THE MOST TODAY

3 THINGS I WISH FOR TOMORROW

○
○
○

DATE: /   /

WO RISKS. WO MAGIC

TOP 3 THIGS ABOUT TODAY

○ _______________________
○ _______________________
○ _______________________

WHAT EMOTIONS HAVE YOU FELT TODAY!

HOW WOULD YOU RATE THE DAY!

☆ ☆ ☆ ☆ ☆

WHAT INSPIRED YOU THE MOST TODAY!

3 THINGS I WISH FOR TOMORROW

○ _______________________
○ _______________________
○ _______________________

DATE: /   /

TOP 3 THINGS ABOUT TODAY
- ○
- ○
- ○

WHAT EMOTIONS HAVE YOU FELT TODAY?

HOW WOULD YOU RATE THE DAY?

☆ ☆ ☆ ☆ ☆

WHAT INSPIRED YOU THE MOST TODAY?

3 THINGS I WISH FOR TOMORROW
- ○
- ○
- ○

DATE: /   /

TOP 3 THINGS ABOUT TODAY

○ __________________________

○ __________________________

○ __________________________

WHAT EMOTIONS HAVE YOU FELT TODAY?

HOW WOULD YOU RATE THE DAY?

☆ ☆ ☆ ☆ ☆

WHAT INSPIRED YOU THE MOST TODAY?

3 THINGS I WISH FOR TOMORROW

○ __________________________

○ __________________________

○ __________________________

DATE: /   /

NO RISKS. NO MAGIC

TOP 3 THINGS ABOUT TODAY
○ __________________
○ __________________
○ __________________

WHAT INSPIRED YOU THE MOST TODAY!

WHAT EMOTIONS HAVE YOU FELT TODAY!

3 THINGS I WISH FOR TOMORROW
○ __________________
○ __________________
○ __________________

HOW WOULD YOU RATE THE DAY!
☆ ☆ ☆ ☆ ☆

DATE: /   /

NO RISKS, NO MAGIC

TOP 3 THINGS ABOUT TODAY
○
○
○

WHAT INSPIRED YOU THE MOST TODAY?

WHAT EMOTIONS HAVE YOU FELT TODAY?

3 THINGS I WISH FOR TOMORROW
○
○
○

HOW WOULD YOU RATE THE DAY?
☆ ☆ ☆ ☆ ☆

DATE: /   /

NO RISKS, NO MAGIC

TOP 3 THINGS ABOUT TODAY
○ ______________________
○ ______________________
○ ______________________

WHAT EMOTIONS HAVE YOU FELT TODAY

HOW WOULD YOU RATE THE DAY

☆ ☆ ☆ ☆ ☆

WHAT INSPIRED YOU THE MOST TODAY

3 THINGS I WISH FOR TOMORROW
○ ______________________
○ ______________________
○ ______________________

DATE: /   /

TOP 3 THINGS ABOUT TODAY

○ __________________________
○ __________________________
○ __________________________

WHAT INSPIRED YOU THE MOST TODAY?

WHAT EMOTIONS HAVE YOU FELT TODAY?

3 THINGS I WISH FOR TOMORROW

○ __________________________
○ __________________________
○ __________________________

HOW WOULD YOU RATE THE DAY?

☆ ☆ ☆ ☆ ☆

DATE: /   /

TOP 3 THINGS ABOUT TODAY
○
○
○

WHAT EMOTIONS HAVE YOU FELT TODAY

HOW WOULD YOU RATE THE DAY

WHAT INSPIRED YOU THE MOST TODAY

3 THINGS I WISH FOR TOMORROW
○
○
○

DATE: / /

WO RISKS. WO MAGIC

TOP 3 THIGS ABOUT TODAY
○ ___________________
○ ___________________
○ ___________________

WHAT EMOTIONS HAVE YOU FELT TODAY!

HOW WOULD YOU RATE THE DAY!

☆ ☆ ☆ ☆ ☆

WHAT INSPIRED YOU THE MOST TODAY!

3 THINGS I WISH FOR TOMORROW
○ ___________________
○ ___________________
○ ___________________

DATE: /   /

TOP 3 THINGS ABOUT TODAY
○ ______________________
○ ______________________
○ ______________________

WHAT EMOTIONS HAVE YOU FELT TODAY?

HOW WOULD YOU RATE THE DAY?
☆ ☆ ☆ ☆ ☆

WHAT INSPIRED YOU THE MOST TODAY?

3 THINGS I WISH FOR TOMORROW
○ ______________________
○ ______________________
○ ______________________

DATE: /   /

NO RISKS. NO MAGIC

TOP 3 THINGS ABOUT TODAY

○
○
○

WHAT INSPIRED YOU THE MOST TODAY?

WHAT EMOTIONS HAVE YOU FELT TODAY?

3 THINGS I WISH FOR TOMORROW

○
○
○

HOW WOULD YOU RATE THE DAY?

DATE: /   /

NO RISKS. NO MAGIC

TOP 3 THIGS ABOUT TODAY

○ _______________________
○ _______________________
○ _______________________

WHAT EMOTIONS HAVE YOU FELT TODAY!

WHAT INSPIRED YOU THE MOST TODAY!

HOW WOULD YOU RATE THE DAY!

☆ ☆ ☆ ☆ ☆

3 THINGS I WISH FOR TOMORROW

○ _______________________
○ _______________________
○ _______________________

DATE: /   /

NO RISKS. NO MAGIC

TOP 3 THINGS ABOUT TODAY

○ ___________________________
○ ___________________________
○ ___________________________

WHAT EMOTIONS HAVE YOU FELT TODAY?

HOW WOULD YOU RATE THE DAY?

☆ ☆ ☆ ☆ ☆

WHAT INSPIRED YOU THE MOST TODAY?

3 THINGS I WISH FOR TOMORROW

○ ___________________________
○ ___________________________
○ ___________________________

____
____
____
____
____

____
____
____
____
____

TOP 3 THINGS ABOUT TODAY
○ ___________________________
○ ___________________________
○ ___________________________

WHAT EMOTIONS HAVE YOU FELT TODAY?
____

HOW WOULD YOU RATE THE DAY?
____
☆ ☆ ☆ ☆ ☆

WHAT INSPIRED YOU THE MOST TODAY?

3 THINGS I WISH FOR TOMORROW
____
○ ___________________________
○ ___________________________
○ ___________________________

NO RISKS. NO MAGIC

TOP 3 THINGS ABOUT TODAY

○
○
○

WHAT EMOTIONS HAVE YOU FELT TODAY?

WHAT INSPIRED YOU THE MOST TODAY?

3 THINGS I WISH FOR TOMORROW

○
○
○

HOW WOULD YOU RATE THE DAY?

☆ ☆ ☆ ☆ ☆

DATE: /   /

TOP 3 THIGS ABOUT TODAY

○ _______________________
○ _______________________
○ _______________________

WHAT EMOTIONS HAVE YOU FELT TODAY!

WHAT INSPIRED YOU THE MOST TODAY!

3 THINGS I WISH FOR TOMORROW

○ _______________________
○ _______________________
○ _______________________

HOW WOULD YOU RATE THE DAY!

☆ ☆ ☆ ☆ ☆

TOP 3 THINGS ABOUT TODAY

○ ____________________

○ ____________________

○ ____________________

WHAT EMOTIONS HAVE YOU FELT TODAY?

HOW WOULD YOU RATE THE DAY?

WHAT INSPIRED YOU THE MOST TODAY?

3 THINGS I WISH FOR TOMORROW

○ ____________________

○ ____________________

○ ____________________

DATE: /   /

TOP 3 THINGS ABOUT TODAY

○ _______________________
○ _______________________
○ _______________________

WHAT EMOTIONS HAVE YOU FELT TODAY

HOW WOULD YOU RATE THE DAY

☆ ☆ ☆ ☆ ☆

WHAT INSPIRED YOU THE MOST TODAY

3 THINGS I WISH FOR TOMORROW

○ _______________________
○ _______________________
○ _______________________

DATE: /   /

TOP 3 THINGS ABOUT TODAY
○ ________________________
○ ________________________
○ ________________________

WHAT EMOTIONS HAVE YOU FELT TODAY?

HOW WOULD YOU RATE THE DAY?
☆ ☆ ☆ ☆ ☆

WHAT INSPIRED YOU THE MOST TODAY?

3 THINGS I WISH FOR TOMORROW
○ ________________________
○ ________________________
○ ________________________

DATE: /   /

NO RISKS. NO MAGIC

TOP 3 THINGS ABOUT TODAY
○
○
○

WHAT EMOTIONS HAVE YOU FELT TODAY?

HOW WOULD YOU RATE THE DAY?

☆ ☆ ☆ ☆ ☆

WHAT INSPIRED YOU THE MOST TODAY?

3 THINGS I WISH FOR TOMORROW
○
○
○

DATE: /   /

NO RISKS, NO MAGIC

TOP 3 THINGS ABOUT TODAY

○ ____________________________

○ ____________________________

○ ____________________________

WHAT INSPIRED YOU THE MOST TODAY?

WHAT EMOTIONS HAVE YOU FELT TODAY?

3 THINGS I WISH FOR TOMORROW

○ ____________________________

○ ____________________________

○ ____________________________

HOW WOULD YOU RATE THE DAY?

☆ ☆ ☆ ☆ ☆

DATE: /   /

NO RISKS. NO MAGIC

TOP 3 THINGS ABOUT TODAY
○ ____________________
○ ____________________
○ ____________________

WHAT INSPIRED YOU THE MOST TODAY?

WHAT EMOTIONS HAVE YOU FELT TODAY?

3 THINGS I WISH FOR TOMORROW
○ ____________________
○ ____________________
○ ____________________

HOW WOULD YOU RATE THE DAY?

☆ ☆ ☆ ☆ ☆

DATE: /   /

TOP 3 THINGS ABOUT TODAY
○
○
○

WHAT INSPIRED YOU THE MOST TODAY?

WHAT EMOTIONS HAVE YOU FELT TODAY?

3 THINGS I WISH FOR TOMORROW
○
○
○

HOW WOULD YOU RATE THE DAY?
☆ ☆ ☆ ☆ ☆

DATE: /   /

WO RISKS, WO MAGIC

TOP 3 THIGS ABOUT TODAY
○
○
○

WHAT INSPIRED YOU THE MOST TODAY

WHAT EMOTIONS HAVE YOU FELT TODAY

3 THINGS I WISH FOR TOMORROW
○
○
○

HOW WOULD YOU RATE THE DAY

NO RISKS, NO MAGIC

TOP 3 THINGS ABOUT TODAY

○ ______________________
○ ______________________
○ ______________________

WHAT EMOTIONS HAVE YOU FELT TODAY?

HOW WOULD YOU RATE THE DAY?

☆ ☆ ☆ ☆ ☆

WHAT INSPIRED YOU THE MOST TODAY?

3 THINGS I WISH FOR TOMORROW

○ ______________________
○ ______________________
○ ______________________

DATE: /   /

TOP 3 THINGS ABOUT TODAY
○
○
○

WHAT INSPIRED YOU THE MOST TODAY?

WHAT EMOTIONS HAVE YOU FELT TODAY?

3 THINGS I WISH FOR TOMORROW
○
○
○

HOW WOULD YOU RATE THE DAY?
☆ ☆ ☆ ☆ ☆

DATE: /   /

TOP 3 THIGS ABOUT TODAY

○

○

○

WHAT EMOTIONS HAVE YOU FELT TODAY!

HOW WOULD YOU RATE THE DAY!

WHAT INSPIRED YOU THE MOST TODAY!

3 THINGS I WISH FOR TOMORROW

○

○

○

DATE: /   /

TOP 3 THIGS ABOUT TODAY
○ __________________________
○ __________________________
○ __________________________

WHAT INSPIRED YOU THE MOST TODAY?

WHAT EMOTIONS HAVE YOU FELT TODAY?

3 THINGS I WISH FOR TOMORROW
○ __________________________
○ __________________________
○ __________________________

HOW WOULD YOU RATE THE DAY?

☆ ☆ ☆ ☆ ☆

____
____
____
____
____
____

____
____
____
____
____

NO RISKS. NO MAGIC

TOP 3 THINGS ABOUT TODAY

○ ______________________________
○ ______________________________
○ ______________________________

WHAT EMOTIONS HAVE YOU FELT TODAY!

HOW WOULD YOU RATE THE DAY!

☆ ☆ ☆ ☆ ☆

WHAT INSPIRED YOU THE MOST TODAY!

3 THINGS I WISH FOR TOMORROW

○ ______________________________
○ ______________________________
○ ______________________________

DATE: /   /

NO RISKS. NO MAGIC

TOP 3 THINGS ABOUT TODAY
○ _______________________
○ _______________________
○ _______________________

WHAT EMOTIONS HAVE YOU FELT TODAY?

HOW WOULD YOU RATE THE DAY?

☆ ☆ ☆ ☆ ☆

WHAT INSPIRED YOU THE MOST TODAY?

3 THINGS I WISH FOR TOMORROW
○ _______________________
○ _______________________
○ _______________________

DATE: /   /

NO RISKS. NO MAGIC

TOP 3 THINGS ABOUT TODAY
○
○
○

WHAT INSPIRED YOU THE MOST TODAY?

WHAT EMOTIONS HAVE YOU FELT TODAY?

3 THINGS I WISH FOR TOMORROW
○
○
○

HOW WOULD YOU RATE THE DAY?

☆ ☆ ☆ ☆ ☆

NO RISKS. NO MAGIC

TOP 3 THINGS ABOUT TODAY
○ _______________
○ _______________
○ _______________

WHAT EMOTIONS HAVE YOU FELT TODAY?

HOW WOULD YOU RATE THE DAY?
☆ ☆ ☆ ☆ ☆

WHAT INSPIRED YOU THE MOST TODAY?

3 THINGS I WISH FOR TOMORROW
○ _______________
○ _______________
○ _______________

NO RISKS, NO MAGIC

TOP 3 THINGS ABOUT TODAY
- ○
- ○
- ○

WHAT EMOTIONS HAVE YOU FELT TODAY?

HOW WOULD YOU RATE THE DAY?
☆ ☆ ☆ ☆ ☆

WHAT INSPIRED YOU THE MOST TODAY?

3 THINGS I WISH FOR TOMORROW
- ○
- ○
- ○

DATE: /   /

TOP 3 THINGS ABOUT TODAY

○ ____________________
○ ____________________
○ ____________________

WHAT EMOTIONS HAVE YOU FELT TODAY?

HOW WOULD YOU RATE THE DAY?

☆ ☆ ☆ ☆ ☆

WHAT INSPIRED YOU THE MOST TODAY?

3 THINGS I WISH FOR TOMORROW

○ ____________________
○ ____________________
○ ____________________

DATE: /   /

NO RISKS. NO MAGIC

TOP 3 THINGS ABOUT TODAY
○ ___________________________
○ ___________________________
○ ___________________________

WHAT EMOTIONS HAVE YOU FELT TODAY?

HOW WOULD YOU RATE THE DAY?

☆ ☆ ☆ ☆ ☆

WHAT INSPIRED YOU THE MOST TODAY?

3 THINGS I WISH FOR TOMORROW
○ ___________________________
○ ___________________________
○ ___________________________

DATE: /   /

No RISKS. No MAGIC

____
____
____
____
____
____
____
____
____

TOP 3 THINGS ABOUT TODAY
○ ________________________________
○ ________________________________
○ ________________________________

WHAT EMOTIONS HAVE YOU FELT TODAY?

WHAT INSPIRED YOU THE MOST TODAY?

3 THINGS I WISH FOR TOMORROW
○ ________________________________
○ ________________________________
○ ________________________________

HOW WOULD YOU RATE THE DAY?

☆ ☆ ☆ ☆ ☆

DATE   /   /

NO RISKS. NO MAGIC

TOP 3 THINGS ABOUT TODAY

○ ______________________
○ ______________________
○ ______________________

WHAT EMOTIONS HAVE YOU FELT TODAY?

HOW WOULD YOU RATE THE DAY?

☆ ☆ ☆ ☆ ☆

WHAT INSPIRED YOU THE MOST TODAY?

3 THINGS I WISH FOR TOMORROW

○ ______________________
○ ______________________
○ ______________________

DATE: /   /

NO RISKS. NO MAGIC

TOP 3 THINGS ABOUT TODAY
○
○
○

WHAT INSPIRED YOU THE MOST TODAY?

WHAT EMOTIONS HAVE YOU FELT TODAY?

3 THINGS I WISH FOR TOMORROW
○
○
○

HOW WOULD YOU RATE THE DAY?
☆ ☆ ☆ ☆ ☆

DATE: / /

TOP 3 THIGS ABOUT TODAY

○ ____________________
○ ____________________
○ ____________________

WHAT INSPIRED YOU THE MOST TODAY?

WHAT EMOTIONS HAVE YOU FELT TODAY?

3 THINGS I WISH FOR TOMORROW

○ ____________________
○ ____________________
○ ____________________

HOW WOULD YOU RATE THE DAY?

☆ ☆ ☆ ☆ ☆

DATE: /   /

NO RISKS. NO MAGIC

TOP 3 THINGS ABOUT TODAY
○ _______________________
○ _______________________
○ _______________________

WHAT EMOTIONS HAVE YOU FELT TODAY!

HOW WOULD YOU RATE THE DAY!
☆ ☆ ☆ ☆ ☆

WHAT INSPIRED YOU THE MOST TODAY!

3 THINGS I WISH FOR TOMORROW
○ _______________________
○ _______________________
○ _______________________

DATE: /   /

NO RISKS, NO MAGIC

TOP 3 THINGS ABOUT TODAY

○

○

○

WHAT INSPIRED YOU THE MOST TODAY?

WHAT EMOTIONS HAVE YOU FELT TODAY?

3 THINGS I WISH FOR TOMORROW

○

○

○

HOW WOULD YOU RATE THE DAY?

☆ ☆ ☆ ☆ ☆

DATE: /   /

TOP 3 THINGS ABOUT TODAY
-
-
-

WHAT EMOTIONS HAVE YOU FELT TODAY

HOW WOULD YOU RATE THE DAY

WHAT INSPIRED YOU THE MOST TODAY

3 THINGS I WISH FOR TOMORROW
-
-
-

DATE: /   /

NO RISKS. NO MAGIC

TOP 3 THINGS ABOUT TODAY
○ _______________________
○ _______________________
○ _______________________

WHAT INSPIRED YOU THE MOST TODAY?

WHAT EMOTIONS HAVE YOU FELT TODAY?

3 THINGS I WISH FOR TOMORROW
○ _______________________
○ _______________________
○ _______________________

HOW WOULD YOU RATE THE DAY?

☆ ☆ ☆ ☆ ☆

DATE: _____ / _____ / _____

____
____
____
____
____
____
____
____
____

NO RISKS, NO MAGIC

TOP 3 THINGS ABOUT TODAY
○ _______________________________
○ _______________________________
○ _______________________________

WHAT EMOTIONS HAVE YOU FELT TODAY?

HOW WOULD YOU RATE THE DAY?
☆ ☆ ☆ ☆ ☆

WHAT INSPIRED YOU THE MOST TODAY?

3 THINGS I WISH FOR TOMORROW
○ _______________________________
○ _______________________________
○ _______________________________

DATE: / /

NO RISKS. NO MAGIC

TOP 3 THIGS ABOUT TODAY

○
○
○

WHAT INSPIRED YOU THE MOST TODAY

WHAT EMOTIONS HAVE YOU FELT TODAY

3 THINGS I WISH FOR TOMORROW

○
○
○

HOW WOULD YOU RATE THE DAY

DATE: /   /

TOP 3 THINGS ABOUT TODAY
○
○
○

WHAT INSPIRED YOU THE MOST TODAY?

WHAT EMOTIONS HAVE YOU FELT TODAY?

3 THINGS I WISH FOR TOMORROW
○
○
○

HOW WOULD YOU RATE THE DAY?
☆ ☆ ☆ ☆ ☆

DATE: /   /

NO RISKS. NO MAGIC

TOP 3 THINGS ABOUT TODAY

○ ___________________________
○ ___________________________
○ ___________________________

WHAT INSPIRED YOU THE MOST TODAY?

WHAT EMOTIONS HAVE YOU FELT TODAY?

3 THINGS I WISH FOR TOMORROW

○ ___________________________
○ ___________________________
○ ___________________________

HOW WOULD YOU RATE THE DAY?

☆ ☆ ☆ ☆ ☆

DATE: /   /

WO RISKS. WO MAGIC

TOP 3 THIGS ABOUT TODAY
○
○
○

WHAT EMOTIONS HAVE YOU FELT TODAY

HOW WOULD YOU RATE THE DAY?

WHAT INSPIRED YOU THE MOST TODAY?

3 THINGS I WISH FOR TOMORROW
○
○
○

NO RISKS. NO MAGIC

TOP 3 THINGS ABOUT TODAY

○ _______________________________
○ _______________________________
○ _______________________________

WHAT EMOTIONS HAVE YOU FELT TODAY?

HOW WOULD YOU RATE THE DAY?

☆ ☆ ☆ ☆ ☆

WHAT INSPIRED YOU THE MOST TODAY?

3 THINGS I WISH FOR TOMORROW

○ _______________________________
○ _______________________________
○ _______________________________

DATE: /   /

TOP 3 THINGS ABOUT TODAY
○
○
○

WHAT EMOTIONS HAVE YOU FELT TODAY?

HOW WOULD YOU RATE THE DAY?

WHAT INSPIRED YOU THE MOST TODAY?

3 THINGS I WISH FOR TOMORROW
○
○
○

DATE: / /

TOP 3 THIGS ABOUT TODAY

○

○

○

WHAT EMOTIONS HAVE YOU FELT TODAY?

HOW WOULD YOU RATE THE DAY?

☆ ☆ ☆ ☆ ☆

WHAT INSPIRED YOU THE MOST TODAY?

3 THINGS I WISH FOR TOMORROW

○

○

○

TOP 3 THIGS ABOUT TODAY
○
○
○

WHAT INSPIRED YOU THE MOST TODAY!

WHAT EMOTIONS HAVE YOU FELT TODAY!

3 THINGS I WISH FOR TOMORROW
○
○
○

HOW WOULD YOU RATE THE DAY!
☆ ☆ ☆ ☆ ☆

DATE: /   /

NO RISKS. NO MAGIC

TOP 3 THINGS ABOUT TODAY

○ ___________________________

○ ___________________________

○ ___________________________

WHAT INSPIRED YOU THE MOST TODAY?

WHAT EMOTIONS HAVE YOU FELT TODAY?

3 THINGS I WISH FOR TOMORROW

○ ___________________________

○ ___________________________

○ ___________________________

HOW WOULD YOU RATE THE DAY?

☆ ☆ ☆ ☆ ☆

DATE: /   /

WO RISKS. WO MAGIC

TOP 3 THIGS ABOUT TODAY

○ ___________________________

○ ___________________________

○ ___________________________

WHAT INSPIRED YOU THE MOST TODAY?

WHAT EMOTIONS HAVE YOU FELT TODAY?

3 THINGS I WISH FOR TOMORROW

○ ___________________________

○ ___________________________

○ ___________________________

HOW WOULD YOU RATE THE DAY?

☆ ☆ ☆ ☆ ☆

DATE: /   /

____

TOP 3 THINGS ABOUT TODAY
○ _______________________________
○ _______________________________
○ _______________________________

WHAT EMOTIONS HAVE YOU FELT TODAY?

HOW WOULD YOU RATE THE DAY?
☆ ☆ ☆ ☆ ☆

WHAT INSPIRED YOU THE MOST TODAY?

3 THINGS I WISH FOR TOMORROW
○ _______________________________
○ _______________________________
○ _______________________________

DATE: /   /

TOP 3 THIGS ABOUT TODAY

○ _______________________

○ _______________________

○ _______________________

WHAT EMOTIONS HAVE YOU FELT TODAY!

HOW WOULD YOU RATE THE DAY!

☆ ☆ ☆ ☆ ☆

WHAT INSPIRED YOU THE MOST TODAY!

3 THINGS I WISH FOR TOMORROW

○ _______________________

○ _______________________

○ _______________________

DATE: /   /

TOP 3 THINGS ABOUT TODAY

○ ___________________________________

○ ___________________________________

○ ___________________________________

WHAT EMOTIONS HAVE YOU FELT TODAY?

HOW WOULD YOU RATE THE DAY?

☆ ☆ ☆ ☆ ☆

WHAT INSPIRED YOU THE MOST TODAY?

3 THINGS I WISH FOR TOMORROW

○ ___________________________________

○ ___________________________________

○ ___________________________________

DATE: /   /

NO RISKS. NO MAGIC

TOP 3 THIGS ABOUT TODAY
○
○
○

WHAT EMOTIONS HAVE YOU FELT TODAY?

HOW WOULD YOU RATE THE DAY?

WHAT INSPIRED YOU THE MOST TODAY?

3 THINGS I WISH FOR TOMORROW
○
○
○

DATE: /   /

____

TOP 3 THINGS ABOUT TODAY

○ ___________________________
○ ___________________________
○ ___________________________

WHAT EMOTIONS HAVE YOU FELT TODAY?

HOW WOULD YOU RATE THE DAY?

☆ ☆ ☆ ☆ ☆

WHAT INSPIRED YOU THE MOST TODAY?

3 THINGS I WISH FOR TOMORROW

○ ___________________________
○ ___________________________
○ ___________________________

DATE: /   /

WO RISKS. WO MAGIC

TOP 3 THIGS ABOUT TODAY
○
○
○

WHAT INSPIRED YOU THE MOST TODAY

WHAT EMOTIONS HAVE YOU FELT TODAY

3 THINGS I WISH FOR TOMORROW
○
○
○

HOW WOULD YOU RATE THE DAY
☆ ☆ ☆ ☆ ☆

DATE: /   /

NO RISKS. NO MAGIC

TOP 3 THINGS ABOUT TODAY
○
○
○

WHAT INSPIRED YOU THE MOST TODAY?

WHAT EMOTIONS HAVE YOU FELT TODAY?

3 THINGS I WISH FOR TOMORROW
○
○
○

HOW WOULD YOU RATE THE DAY?

☆ ☆ ☆ ☆ ☆

DATE: /   /

NO RISKS. NO MAGIC

TOP 3 THIGS ABOUT TODAY
○ _______________________
○ _______________________
○ _______________________

WHAT EMOTIONS HAVE YOU FELT TODAY!

HOW WOULD YOU RATE THE DAY!

☆ ☆ ☆ ☆ ☆

WHAT INSPIRED YOU THE MOST TODAY!

3 THINGS I WISH FOR TOMORROW
○ _______________________
○ _______________________
○ _______________________

DATE: /   /

TOP 3 THINGS ABOUT TODAY
○
○
○

WHAT EMOTIONS HAVE YOU FELT TODAY?

HOW WOULD YOU RATE THE DAY?
☆ ☆ ☆ ☆ ☆

WHAT INSPIRED YOU THE MOST TODAY?

3 THINGS I WISH FOR TOMORROW
○
○
○

DATE: /   /

NO RISKS. NO MAGIC

TOP 3 THIGS ABOUT TODAY
○
○
○

WHAT INSPIRED YOU THE MOST TODAY

WHAT EMOTIONS HAVE YOU FELT TODAY

3 THINGS I WISH FOR TOMORROW
○
○
○

HOW WOULD YOU RATE THE DAY

☆ ☆ ☆ ☆ ☆

DATE: /   /

WO RISKS. WO MAGIC

TOP 3 THIGS ABOUT TODAY
○
○
○

WHAT INSPIRED YOU THE MOST TODAY?

WHAT EMOTIONS HAVE YOU FELT TODAY?

3 THINGS I WISH FOR TOMORROW
○
○
○

HOW WOULD YOU RATE THE DAY?
☆ ☆ ☆ ☆ ☆

DATE: /   /

NO RISKS. NO MAGIC

TOP 3 THINGS ABOUT TODAY

○

○

○

WHAT INSPIRED YOU THE MOST TODAY?

WHAT EMOTIONS HAVE YOU FELT TODAY?

3 THINGS I WISH FOR TOMORROW

○

○

○

HOW WOULD YOU RATE THE DAY?

☆ ☆ ☆ ☆ ☆

DATE: /   /

NO RISKS. NO MAGIC

TOP 3 THINGS ABOUT TODAY

○ _______________________

○ _______________________

○ _______________________

WHAT INSPIRED YOU THE MOST TODAY!

WHAT EMOTIONS HAVE YOU FELT TODAY!

3 THINGS I WISH FOR TOMORROW

○ _______________________

○ _______________________

○ _______________________

HOW WOULD YOU RATE THE DAY!

☆ ☆ ☆ ☆ ☆

____

DATE: /   /

____
____
____
____
____

____
____
____
____
____

TOP 3 THINGS ABOUT TODAY
○ ________________________
○ ________________________
○ ________________________

WHAT INSPIRED YOU THE MOST TODAY?

WHAT EMOTIONS HAVE YOU FELT TODAY?
____

3 THINGS I WISH FOR TOMORROW
____
○ ________________________
○ ________________________
○ ________________________

HOW WOULD YOU RATE THE DAY?
____
☆ ☆ ☆ ☆ ☆

DATE: /   /

NO RISKS, NO MAGIC

TOP 3 THINGS ABOUT TODAY
○
○
○

WHAT INSPIRED YOU THE MOST TODAY?

WHAT EMOTIONS HAVE YOU FELT TODAY?

3 THINGS I WISH FOR TOMORROW
○
○
○

HOW WOULD YOU RATE THE DAY?
☆ ☆ ☆ ☆ ☆

DATE: /   /

NO RISKS. NO MAGIC

TOP 3 THINGS ABOUT TODAY
○
○
○

WHAT INSPIRED YOU THE MOST TODAY?

WHAT EMOTIONS HAVE YOU FELT TODAY?

3 THINGS I WISH FOR TOMORROW
○
○
○

HOW WOULD YOU RATE THE DAY?
☆ ☆ ☆ ☆ ☆

NO RISKS. NO MAGIC

TOP 3 THINGS ABOUT TODAY

○

○

○

WHAT INSPIRED YOU THE MOST TODAY?

WHAT EMOTIONS HAVE YOU FELT TODAY?

3 THINGS I WISH FOR TOMORROW

○

○

○

HOW WOULD YOU RATE THE DAY?

☆ ☆ ☆ ☆ ☆

DATE: /   /

NO RISKS, NO MAGIC

TOP 3 THIGS ABOUT TODAY
○
○
○

WHAT INSPIRED YOU THE MOST TODAY

WHAT EMOTIONS HAVE YOU FELT TODAY

3 THINGS I WISH FOR TOMORROW
○
○
○

HOW WOULD YOU RATE THE DAY

DATE: /   /

NO RISKS. NO MAGIC

TOP 3 THIGS ABOUT TODAY
○
○
○

WHAT INSPIRED YOU THE MOST TODAY?

WHAT EMOTIONS HAVE YOU FELT TODAY?

3 THINGS I WISH FOR TOMORROW
○
○
○

HOW WOULD YOU RATE THE DAY?

☆ ☆ ☆ ☆ ☆

DATE: /   /

NO RISKS, NO MAGIC

TOP 3 THINGS ABOUT TODAY
○ __________________________
○ __________________________
○ __________________________

WHAT EMOTIONS HAVE YOU FELT TODAY?

HOW WOULD YOU RATE THE DAY?
☆ ☆ ☆ ☆ ☆

WHAT INSPIRED YOU THE MOST TODAY?

3 THINGS I WISH FOR TOMORROW
○ __________________________
○ __________________________
○ __________________________

DATE: / /

TOP 3 THINGS ABOUT TODAY

○
○
○

WHAT EMOTIONS HAVE YOU FELT TODAY?

HOW WOULD YOU RATE THE DAY?

☆ ☆ ☆ ☆ ☆

WHAT INSPIRED YOU THE MOST TODAY?

3 THINGS I WISH FOR TOMORROW

○
○
○

DATE: / /

NO RISKS. NO MAGIC

TOP 3 THIGS ABOUT TODAY
○
○
○

WHAT EMOTIONS HAVE YOU FELT TODAY?

HOW WOULD YOU RATE THE DAY?

WHAT INSPIRED YOU THE MOST TODAY?

3 THINGS I WISH FOR TOMORROW
○
○
○

DATE: /   /

TOP 3 THINGS ABOUT TODAY

○ _______________________________

○ _______________________________

○ _______________________________

WHAT EMOTIONS HAVE YOU FELT TODAY?

HOW WOULD YOU RATE THE DAY?

☆ ☆ ☆ ☆ ☆

WHAT INSPIRED YOU THE MOST TODAY?

3 THINGS I WISH FOR TOMORROW

○ _______________________________

○ _______________________________

○ _______________________________

DATE: /   /

TOP 3 THIGS ABOUT TODAY
○ _______________________
○ _______________________
○ _______________________

WHAT EMOTIONS HAVE YOU FELT TODAY?

HOW WOULD YOU RATE THE DAY?

☆ ☆ ☆ ☆ ☆

WHAT INSPIRED YOU THE MOST TODAY?

3 THINGS I WISH FOR TOMORROW
○ _______________________
○ _______________________
○ _______________________

DATE: /   /

TOP 3 THINGS ABOUT TODAY
○
○
○

WHAT EMOTIONS HAVE YOU FELT TODAY?

HOW WOULD YOU RATE THE DAY?
☆ ☆ ☆ ☆ ☆

WHAT INSPIRED YOU THE MOST TODAY?

3 THINGS I WISH FOR TOMORROW
○
○
○

DATE: /   /

NO RISKS. NO MAGIC

TOP 3 THINGS ABOUT TODAY

○ _______________________

○ _______________________

○ _______________________

WHAT EMOTIONS HAVE YOU FELT TODAY?

HOW WOULD YOU RATE THE DAY?

☆ ☆ ☆ ☆ ☆

WHAT INSPIRED YOU THE MOST TODAY?

3 THINGS I WISH FOR TOMORROW

○ _______________________

○ _______________________

○ _______________________

DATE: /   /

TOP 3 THIGS ABOUT TODAY

○ ______________________

○ ______________________

○ ______________________

WHAT EMOTIONS HAVE YOU FELT TODAY?

WHAT INSPIRED YOU THE MOST TODAY?

3 THINGS I WISH FOR TOMORROW

○ ______________________

○ ______________________

○ ______________________

HOW WOULD YOU RATE THE DAY?

☆ ☆ ☆ ☆ ☆